Handling kids with autism
Effective guide on how to know, understand and love kids with autism

Table of content

Chapter one

What is autism

Autism spectrum disorders (ASD) are a wide range of illnesses. They are distinguished by some degree of difficulties with social contact and communication. Other features include aberrant patterns of activities and behaviors, such as trouble with the transition from one task to another, a concentration on minutiae, and unexpected responses to stimuli.

The talents and demands of autistic persons vary and might grow over time. While some persons with autism may live independently, others have significant difficulties and need life-long care and assistance. Autism frequently influences education and job chances. In addition, the responsibilities of families providing care and assistance might be enormous. Societal views and the degree of assistance offered by local and national authorities are major variables impacting the quality of life of persons with autism.

Characteristics of autism may be noticed in early infancy, however, autism is frequently not diagnosed until much later.

People with autism frequently have co-occurring disorders, including epilepsy, depression, anxiety, and attention deficit hyperactivity disorder as well as problematic habits such as difficulties sleeping and self-injury. The degree of intellectual functioning among autistic persons varies greatly, going from severe disability to exceptional levels.

Epidemiology
It is believed that globally roughly one in 100 children has autism. This estimate reflects an average value because reported prevalence varies greatly among research. Some well-controlled studies have, however, revealed much higher numbers. The

frequency of autism in many low- and middle-income nations is uncertain.

Causes
Available scientific research reveals that there are probably several variables that make a kid more likely to develop autism, including environmental and genetic factors.

Available epidemiological statistics show that there is no indication of a causal relationship between measles, mumps, rubella immunization, and autism. Previous research proposing a causal association was shown to be replete with methodological problems.

There is also no evidence to show that any other childhood immunization may enhance the risk of autism. Evidence evaluations of the possible relationship between the preservative thiomersal and aluminum adjuvants present in inactivated vaccinations and the risk of autism firmly indicated that vaccines do not raise the risk of autism.

Assessment and care

A comprehensive variety of therapies, from early infancy and over the life span, may maximize the development, health, well-being, and quality of life of autistic persons. Timely access to early evidence-based psychosocial therapies may increase the capacity of autistic children to speak effectively and engage socially. The monitoring of child development as part of normal maternal and child health care is suggested.

It is crucial that, after autism has been identified, children, adolescents, and adults with autism and their caregivers be provided appropriate information, services, referrals, and practical assistance, in line with their particular and growing requirements and preferences.

The healthcare requirements of persons with autism are complicated and need a spectrum of integrated services, that include health promotion, treatment, and rehabilitation. Collaboration between the health sector and other sectors, notably education, employment, and social care, is vital.

Interventions for persons with autism and other developmental disorders need to be created and administered with the cooperation of those living with these conditions. Care has to be supplemented by efforts at the community and societal levels for increased accessibility, inclusion, and support.

Human rights
All persons, including those with autism, have the right to the enjoyment of the greatest possible degree of bodily and mental health.

And yet, autistic persons are frequently exposed to stigma and prejudice, including unfair restrictions on health care, education, and chances to interact and contribute to their communities.

People with autism suffer the same health concerns as the general population. However, they may, in addition, have particular health-care requirements due to autism or other co-occurring illnesses. They may be more sensitive to acquiring chronic noncommunicable disorders due to behavioral risk factors such as physical inactivity and poor food habits and are at increased risk of assault, injury, and abuse.

People with autism need accessible health services for general health-care requirements like the rest of the population, including promotive and preventive services and treatment of acute and chronic disease. Nevertheless, autistic persons have greater rates of unmet health-care demands compared with the general population. They are also more susceptible to humanitarian catastrophes. A major obstacle is generated by healthcare providers' insufficient knowledge and comprehension of autism.

Autistic persons may behave differently from normal people
Autistic persons may:\sfind it hard to communicate and engage with other people
find it hard to grasp how other people think or feel\sfind things like bright lights or loud sounds overwhelming, distressing, or uncomfortable
become scared or irritated about unknown circumstances and social gatherings
take longer to grasp information\sdo or think the same things again and over\sInformation:\sIf you believe you or your child may be autistic, receive guidance on the symptoms of autism.

Being autistic does not imply you have a sickness or condition. It distinctly indicates your brain functions from other individuals.

It's something you're born with or initially emerges when you're quite young.

If you're autistic, you're autistic your entire life.

Autism is not a medical illness with therapies or a "cure". But some folks require assistance to aid them with specific tasks.

Autistic persons may live a fulfilling life
Being autistic does not have to stop you from having a nice life.

Like everyone, autistic persons have things they're excellent at as well as things they struggle with.

Being autistic does not imply you can never meet friends, have relationships or obtain a career. But you may need additional support with these items.

Autism is different for everyone
Autism is a spectrum. This implies each with autism is different.

Some autistic persons require little or no help. Others may require aid from a parent or caretaker every day.

Some individuals use different names for autism
There are alternative names for autism used by certain individuals, such as:
autism spectrum disorder (ASD) – the medical term for autism\sautism spectrum condition (ASC) – used instead of ASD by certain individuals
Asperger's (or Asperger syndrome) - is used by some individuals to denote autistic persons with ordinary or above-average intelligence

More about Asperger's
It's not understood what causes autism
Nobody knows what causes autism, or whether it has a cause.

It may affect persons in the same family. So it may occasionally be handed on to a kid by their parents.

Autism is not caused by:
Bad Parenting\svaccines, such as the MMR vaccine\sdiet\san virus you may pass to other people
Autistic persons may have any degree of intellect
Some autistic persons have normal or above-average intellect.

Some autistic persons have learning difficulties. This implies they may find it hard to care for themselves and require support with everyday living.

What Are the Signs of Autism?

Symptoms of autism commonly develop before a kid is 3. Some individuals display indications from birth.

Common signs of autism include:
A lack of eye contact
A restricted range of interests or keen interest in some themes
Doing something again and over, such as repeating words or phrases, swaying back and forth, or flicking a lever
High sensitivity to noises, sensations, scents, or images that appear common to other individuals
Not looking at or listening to other people
Not looking at items when another person points to them
Not wanting to be held or hugged
Problems comprehending or utilizing words, gestures, facial expressions, or tone of voice
Talking in a sing-song, flat, or robotic voice
Trouble adjusting to changes in routine

Some children with autism may also experience seizures. These may not start until adolescence.

What Are the Types of Autism Spectrum Disorders?
These categories were formerly regarded to constitute different conditions. Now, they come within the group of autism spectrum disorders including:

Asperger's syndrome. These youngsters don't have difficulty with language; in fact, they tend to score in the average or above-average range on IQ tests. But they have social issues and a restricted area of interest.

Autistic disorder. This is what most people think of when they hear the term "autism." It refers to issues with social relationships, communication, and play in children younger than 3 years.

Childhood disintegrative disorder. These youngsters experience regular growth for at least 2 years and then lose part or most of their verbal and social abilities.

Pervasive developmental disorder (PDD or atypical autism) (PDD or atypical autism). Your doctor could use this phrase if your kid displays some autistic characteristics, such as deficits in social and communicative abilities, but doesn't fall into another group.

Autism is four times as frequent in males than in girls. It may happen in persons of any race, ethnicity, or socioeconomic status. Family income, lifestyle, or educational level doesn't alter a child's chance of autism. But there are several risk factors:

Autism runs in families, so specific combinations of genes may raise a child's risk.
A kid with an older parent has an increased chance of autism.

Pregnant women who are exposed to particular medicines or chemicals, such as alcohol or anti-seizure medications, are more likely to produce autistic children. Other risk factors include maternal metabolic disorders like as diabetes and obesity. Research has also connected autism to untreated phenylketonuria (commonly called PKU, a metabolic condition caused by the lack of an enzyme) and rubella (German measles) (German measles).

There is no proof that immunizations cause autism.

How Is Autism Diagnosed?
It might be challenging to receive a definitive diagnosis of autism. Your doctor will concentrate on behavior and growth.
For children, diagnosis normally involves two phases.

A developmental screening will inform your doctor if your kid is on track with fundamental skills including learning, speaking, behaving, and mobility. Experts advise that children be evaluated for these developmental delays during their routine checkups at 9 months, 18 months, and 24 or 30 months of age. Children are frequently screened particularly for autism during their 18-month and 24-month exams.

If your kid exhibits indicators of a problem on these exams, they'll require a more extensive assessment. This can involve hearing and vision exams or genetic studies. Your doctor may want to bring in someone who specializes in autistic issues, such as a developmental pediatrician or a child psychologist. Some psychologists may also offer a test called the Autism Diagnostic Observation Schedule (ADOS) (ADOS).

If you weren't diagnosed with autism as a kid but discover yourself displaying indications or symptoms, go to your doctor.

How Is Autism Treated?

There's no cure for autism. But early therapy may make a major impact on the growth of a kid with autism. If you suspect your kid displays indications of ASD, inform your doctor as soon as possible.

What works for one individual may not work for another. Your doctor should customize therapy for you or your kid. The two primary kinds of therapies are:

Behavioral and communication therapy to aid with structure and order. Applied behavior analysis (ABA) is one of these therapies; it encourages good conduct and discourages bad behavior. Occupational therapy may assist with everyday skills including dressing, eating, and interacting with others. Sensory integration therapy could assist someone who has difficulty with being touched or with sights or noises. Speech therapy enhances communication skills.

Medications to aid with symptoms of ASD, such as concentration issues, hyperactivity, or anxiety.

Complementary therapy may assist increase cognitive and communication abilities in certain persons with autism. Complementary treatments include music, painting, or animal therapy, such as horseback riding and even swimming with dolphins.

Be Careful About Changing Your Child's Diet
Talk to your doctor before attempting anything unusual, such as a particular diet. There's no strong evidence that specific diets assist youngsters with ASD. Autism is a complicated neurological condition. While it may appear that taking out particular foods will help your child's symptoms, it can do more damage.

For example, children with autism frequently have smaller bones. Dairy products include nutrients that may make their bones stronger. Studies on a protein in milk products called casein have shown that many youngsters performed the same whether or not they ate meals with this protein. Their autism symptoms didn't alter in any surprising manner.

Some data reveals that persons with autism may have low amounts of certain vitamins and minerals. This does not induce autism spectrum disease. But supplements may be advised to boost nutrition. Vitamin B and magnesium are two of the supplements most often used for people with autism. But humans may overdose on these vitamins, thus megavitamins should be avoided.

However, certain food adjustments may assist with specific symptoms of autism. Food allergies, for example, may make behavior issues worse. Removing the allergen from the diet may help behavior concerns.

The crucial thing is that your child's diet has to accommodate their nutritional demands and ASD symptoms. The greatest strategy to decide on the most effective diet is to work with your doctor and a nutrition consultant like a certified dietitian. They'll help you build a food plan personalized for your kid.

Some children with autism suffer digestive difficulties such as constipation, gut discomfort, nausea, and vomiting. Your doctor can prescribe a diet that won't make them worse.

And remember, nutritional needs change over time. Your child's nutritionist will assist you to make sure the meals they consume are still satisfying their requirements as they become older.

Key facts

Autism – sometimes referred to as autism spectrum disorder–comprises a varied set of problems connected to the development of the brain.

About one in 100 children has autism.

Characteristics may be identified in early infancy, however, autism is frequently not diagnosed until much later.

The talents and demands of autistic persons vary and might grow over time. While some persons with autism may live independently, others have significant difficulties and need life-long care and assistance.

Evidence-based psychosocial therapies may enhance communication and social skills, having a beneficial influence on the well-being and quality of life of both autistic persons and their carers.

Care for persons with autism has to be supplemented by efforts at the community and societal levels for improved accessibility, inclusion, and support.

chapter two

What signs should you look out for

Signs of autism in teens and older children can become visible in school.
Signs include challenges with new social circumstances and abilities at school.
If older children and teens exhibit evidence of autism, start by consulting a GP.
Health experts will diagnose autism only after they've eliminated alternative reasons for children's behaviors.
Signs of autism in older children and teens
Social communication indicators of autism in older children and teens
Behavior symptoms of autism in older children and teens
Other concerns related to autism
Signs of autism in older children and teens
Signs of autism can become visible in school-age children. This is because the school atmosphere may be overpowering and could induce autism indications or make them more noticeable.

In particular, children who are subsequently diagnosed with autism could have problems with social settings at school. For example, kids could find it challenging to follow and take part in discussions correctly, develop friends, and enjoy age-appropriate hobbies.

Some of the primary social communication and behavioral symptoms of autism in middle childhood and adolescence are given below.

If you've seen any of these indicators and/or you're concerned about your child's conduct, consulting your child's GP is extremely essential. The GP may refer your kid to suitable health specialists for examination and diagnosis.

If enough indicators of autism are present, health experts could diagnose your kid with autism. Generally, health experts will establish an autism diagnosis only after they've ruled out other probable reasons for a child's conduct.

Social communication indicators of autism in older children and teens

Older autistic adolescents and teens often have problems utilizing both verbal and nonverbal communication for social goals.

Verbal communication

Older autistic children and teens might:
have problems taking turns in talks - for example, they could want to do all the talking or find it hard to answer inquiries about themselves\sspeak a lot about favored themes, but find it difficult to talk about a variety of issues

be confused by language and interpret things literally — for example, they could be bewildered by the statement 'Pull your socks up!' and pull up their stockings have an odd tone of voice, or uncommonly use speech — for example, they could speak extremely loudly, or in a monotone voice or with an accent\shave very excellent vocabularies and communicate in formal, old-fashioned ways\sfind it hard to follow directions with more than one or two stages.

Nonverbal communication
Older autistic children and teens might:
have trouble reading nonverbal cues, like body language or tone of voice, to guess how someone else is feeling – for example, they might not understand when adults are angry based on their tone of voice, or they might not be able to tell when someone is teasing them or unusually using sarcasm\suse eye contact – for example, they might make less eye contact than others, or not use eye contact when they're spoken to\sexpress few emotions on their faces, or not be able to read other people's facial expressions – for example, they might not be able to tell whether someone likes them in a romantic

way\suse very few gestures to express themselves.

Developing relationships
Older autistic children and teens might:
prefer to spend time on their own, rather than with their peers\sneed other children play by their rules and get upset if their rules aren't followed\shave trouble understanding the social rules of friendship\shave difficulty making friends and have few or no real friends\shave trouble relating to children their age and prefer to play with younger children or adults\shave difficulty adjusting their behavior in different social situations
breach personal space by coming too near to individuals.

Behavior symptoms of autism in older children and teens
Repetitive behaviors and interests
Older autistic children and teens might:

have unusual interests or obsessions – for example, they might collect sticks or memorize football statistics but not be interested in the game\shave compulsive behavior – for example, they might line things up or need to close all the doors in the house\shave an unusual attachment to objects – for example, they might carry toys around, or collect unusual items like chip packets or shoelaces

be easily upset by change and like to follow routines – for example, they might like to sit in the same seat for every meal or have a special order for getting ready in the morning\srepeat body movements or have unusual body movements, like hand-flapping or rocking\smake repetitive noises – for example, grunts, throat-clearing or squealing.

Sensory sensitivity
Older autistic children and teens might:
be sensitive to sensory experiences – for example, they might be easily upset by

certain sounds or uncomfortable clothes, or eat only foods with a certain texture\sseek sensory stimulation – for example, they might like deep pressure, seek vibrating objects like washing machines, or flutter fingers to the sides of their eyes to watch the light flicker\sbe less responsive to pain than other children.

Other concerns related to autism

Older autistic children and teens typically have additional challenges as well. These could include:

difficulties with sleep — for example, they can have difficulty falling asleep, or might routinely wake up or have interrupted sleep patterns

anxiousness or feeling overwhelmed - for example, they can feel apprehensive about traveling to unfamiliar locations, or being in social settings

despair - older autistic children and teens who are conscious of their peculiarities are also typically aware of how others regard them and might feel like outcasts. These emotions of poor mood could be increased by altering hormone levels throughout puberty\sviolent conduct — they commonly have sensory sensitivities that can lead to sudden aggressive behavior.

They could have difficulties comprehending what's going on around them, which can lead to frustration building up\seating disorders — for example, they might have problems shifting to secondary school and might develop an eating disorder to deal with emotions of worry
problems with organization skills – they could find the increase in complexity in secondary school hard to manage\sschool rejection – they might feel overwhelmed or confused at school. They could also be prone to bullying at school
and gender dysphoria - autistic children and teens may be more prone than other children and teenagers to identify as a gender that's different from the sex they

were given at birth. If they feel concerned about this it's called gender dysphoria.

Chapter three

Mode of communication for kids with autism

Communication skills are vital for autistic children's growth. They aid with conduct, learning, and socialization.
Autistic children require help to improve their communication abilities.
To improve your kid's communication abilities, start by identifying the communication level your youngster is utilizing presently.

Communication skills are vital for all youngsters. These abilities let youngsters communicate their needs and wishes. When youngsters can accomplish this, it assists them with behavior, learning, and socializing.

Autistic children have a variety of communication skills and talents. Some autistic children have extremely high communication abilities, but others find it difficult to connect to and interact with other people. Also, some autistic children have difficulty developing language, find it difficult to comprehend or utilize spoken language, or have no language at all.

Autistic children frequently require help to develop and exercise skills for communicating with other people.

Communication is the sharing of ideas, views, or information via voice, writing, or nonverbal expression. Language is communication utilizing words - written, spoken, or signed (as in Auslan) (as in Auslan).

How autistic children communicate
Autistic children often communicate differently from ordinarily developing youngsters. They might:

use language differently

employ non-verbal communication communicate via actions.
Use of language\sAutistic children might:

replicate or repeat other people's words or phrases, or words they've heard on TV, YouTube or videos. They repeat these phrases without meaning or in a strange tone of voice. This is termed echolalia\suse made-up words\ssay the same thing again and over\sconfuse pronouns, referring to themselves as 'you' and the person they're talking to as 'I'.
When autistic children use language in these ways, they could be attempting to communicate. But it might be challenging for other people to grasp what youngsters are trying to convey.

For example, children with echolalia could learn to communicate by repeating words they identify with circumstances or emotional states, learning the meanings of these phrases by finding out how they operate. A youngster could say 'Do you want a lolly?' when they truly want one themselves. This is because when they've heard that question previously, they've had a lollipop.

Over time, many autistic children may build on these beginnings and learn to use language in more conventional ways.

Nonverbal communication
Autistic children might:

physically manipulate a person or object – for example, a child might take a person's hand and push it towards something they want\spoint, show and shift gaze – for example, a child might look at or point to something they want and then shift their gaze to another person, letting that person know they want the object\suse objects – for example, a child might hand an object to another person to communicate.

Conduct\sAutistic children could act in problematic ways, and this behavior is frequently connected to communication.

For example, self-harming behaviors, tantrums, and violence towards others could be a child's way of trying to tell you that they need something, aren't happy, or are genuinely confused or afraid.

If your kid acts in unpleasant ways, attempt to look at things from your child's viewpoint to find out the message underlying your child's actions. Our essay on controlling problematic conduct in autistic children might help you understand why your kid is acting in various ways.

Working on autistic children's communication
It's ideal to work on communication skills for autistic children gradually, by introducing abilities that are only one step from where your kid is present.

You may start by observing your kid closely and recognizing your child's efforts to communicate. This can help you find out what degree of communication your kid is utilizing right now and what step is ideal to teach next.

For example, if your kid cries in the kitchen as a method of asking for food, it can be too hard for your child to learn to speak 'hungry' or 'food'. Instead, the next stage may be training your toddler to point to or reach for the food. You may accomplish this by modeling - that is, teaching your youngster what to do by pointing at the food yourself. You might also assist your kid physically by directing their hand to point at the food.

Or if your kid communicates by pushing your hand towards the items they desire, the next stage may be utilizing words or graphic cards. You might imitate this - for example, by saying 'teddy' or using a 'teddy' image card when your youngster pulls your hand towards their teddy.

When you're working on your child's communication skills, it might help to name objects around your home with words, such as 'bickies', 'train', 'ball', 'brush', and so on.

And it may also assist if you praise your kid each time they utilize the communication skill you're working on.

If you want to work on your autistic child's communication abilities, it's a good idea to receive help from a speech pathologist or other autism specialist. If your kid is receiving NDIS early intervention help or your child has an NDIS plan, you may be eligible to access money for this service.

Making the most of autistic children's efforts to communicate
Here are some ways you may foster communication with your child:

Use brief sentences - for example, 'Shirt on. Hat on.

Use less adult language — for example, 'Playdough feels unpleasant in your mouth.

Exaggerate your tone of voice — for example, 'Ouch, that water is VERY hot.

Encourage and push your kid to fill the gap when it's your child's time in a discussion – for example, 'Look at that dog. What color is the dog?'

Ask inquiries that necessitate a reply from your kid - for example, 'Do you want a sausage?' If you know your kid's response is yes, you may educate your child to nod their head in return by mimicking this for your child.

Give your youngster adequate time to absorb and answer inquiries.

Practice conversing with your youngster on themes or items they're interested in.

Chapter four

Creating an autism friendly home

When you have a child or family member on the autism spectrum, providing a secure and effective home environment is a crucial duty. Autism may have a major influence on an individual's development, lifestyle, and social ties. People on the spectrum might be extremely sensitive to lights, music, and other stimuli. Many want to order and rituals to make sense of the world. Safety might be a worry for persons who wander, are attracted to water, or are prone to head pounding or self-harm.

According to the Autism Society, around 1 percent of the world's population has autism spectrum disorder, and the illness affects about 1 in every 59 children born in the United States. This indicates that in America, 3.5 million individuals are on the autistic spectrum. This number is expanding as diagnostic criteria are becoming more recognized.

Children and adults with autism generally suffer from sensory integration, the neurological process of processing and controlling the sensory information they receive. It might be challenging for them to make sense of sights, sounds, scents, and other sensory information. Three primary sensory systems may be impaired when a person has autism. Understanding these three sensory systems is crucial to understanding persons with autism and how they interact with their home environments:

The tactile system is the sensation of touch, pain, warmth, and pressure
The vestibular system encompasses movement, balance, and head position
The proprioceptive system includes a person's knowledge of the bodily position.
For some persons on the autism spectrum, sensory input is overpowering. They have an

extremely tough time coping with loud or chaotic settings. For others, sensory input is rarely perceived, driving them to want further stimulation. In the autistic community, these two extremes have distinct names. "Sensory seeking" refers to those persons with autism who desire greater sensory stimulation. "Sensory sensitivity" or "sensory avoiding" refers to those persons with autism who are prone to sensory overload, which produces bewilderment, anxiety, and withdrawal.

In any case, for those with autism or sensory processing disorder, living in a world created for neurotypical people may be tough. Thankfully, families that have autistic family members may make their houses more accommodating. Home adaptations, both basic alterations, and more elaborate ones are a fantastic approach to creating a pleasant refuge for persons with autism.

Here is a deeper look at some of the house improvements that might assist someone who is living with autism to feel more comfortable and at ease in the home setting. While many of them are intended for parents with a kid who has autism, they typically apply to adults as well, since the problems of neurodiversity do not have age restrictions.

Consider Visual Stimuli
When a person with autism has a malfunctioning sensory system, the visual information they receive might be difficult to comprehend. Lighting and colors may quickly overwhelm someone with autism. In your house, you may take efforts to limit visual stimuli to diminish this impact, enabling your loved one to feel more comfortable at home. Here are some recommendations to help you achieve this.

Look at the Lighting

Choose lighting that is as similar to natural light as feasible. Lighting comes in varying color temperatures, and particularly sensitive persons may find artificial hues unpleasant. This implies you want to invest in bulbs with a color rendering index (CRI) as near to 100 as feasible.

Avoid lights that flicker. Many forms of artificial lights flicker somewhat. This may not be perceptible to a neurotypical person, but an autistic person may find the flashing insufferable. Fluorescent lighting, especially CFL lighting, typically has difficulties with flickering. LED illumination may eliminate this difficulty.

Consider the sound the lights produce. Lighting may also generate a very low sound, which most people can not hear. Again, the buzz of light might be uncomfortable for someone with autism. Again, fluorescent lighting is a significant cause here.

Install dimmable lights to make it easy to manage the degree of light in the house. This will provide you a degree of control when the intensity of light is too powerful for your autistic loved one, but will enable you to lighten up the environment on days when light sensitivity does not appear to be too severe.

Be conscious of the difficulties brightness might create. Glare from outside sunshine, glare on computer displays, and even glare off of reflecting, hard surfaces, such as hardwood floors, may also be troublesome, so search for solutions to lessen this. Window tinting or anti-glare coatings could assist.

Use Calming Colors
Avoid decorating with loud colors. Many persons with autism perceive colors with higher intensity than neurotypical people. Too many bright colors might be

overstimulating for children and people with autism. Avoid having walls or major items of furniture painted in bright, strong colors. Red, in particular, is too bright and powerful for many persons with autism.

Opt for modest hues, with a neutral color scheme. Pale pink appears to be one of the most relaxing hues for persons with autism. Cool hues are also relaxing.

Use a monochrome color palette. If you install wall hangings on the wall, make them plain without flashy patterns that will intrude on the individual's senses.

Reduce reflections off windows. Whether by the installation of curtains that may filter external light or by adding window film to lessen reflections and glare, identify spots in hour house that might generate distracting and upsetting reflections from windows.

Keep the Home Organized

Reduce the clutter in your house. The confusion generated by clutter makes it harder to function with sensory sensitivity. Go through each area of your home regularly and eliminate unnecessary stuff that is no longer required. This will not only aid your loved one with autism, but it may also ease tension for other family members.

Organize your house to make routines simpler. Children and adults with autism often flourish when they have routines in place. To make things easy for them, keep your house orderly. Establish clear spaces where items belong and put them back promptly after usage.

Install shelves or built-in bookshelves to make storage simpler. Having a place for everything is fundamental to decreasing visual stimulus in the form of clutter. Bookcases with organized storage bins are a useful method to achieve this. Built-in bookshelves may be easily incorporated into the home's design, which will better minimize clutter and increase organization.

Use a container system to make an order and neat living automatic. Separate various sorts of goods and toys, take photographs of them, and paste or clip those images into a container, so they are readily kept and can be retrieved quickly when requested.

Consider Open Concept Home Design
Remove impediments that might block up the line of sight wherever feasible. Open concept floor layouts are simpler for those with sensory processing issues. Removing non-load-bearing walls and opening up the house's floor layout may help make the home more comfortable. This also enables the person with autism to preview a location before entering it, which may increase the individual's comfort in the house.

Avoid cluttering the open concept with too many furnishings. Again, clutter is irritating to persons with autism, so eliminate as much as possible when evaluating the architecture of your floor plan. Arrange furnishings such that your autistic kid may easily shift from one activity to the next without a visual or physical barrier.

Create an in-home walking loop. Once you have an open design, sketch out a walking loop within the house that the person may utilize for pacing habits. Pacing may lower stress greatly, and an open concept design makes this sort of behavior conceivable.

Pay Attention to the Sounds in Your Home
Auditory stimuli may be equally as upsetting as visual stimuli to those with autism. Your house should be a calm haven. Often, children and people with autism may have heightened senses of hearing, and they may pick up on noises that you cannot hear or find themselves uncomfortable with sounds that appear at a normal level to you. This may lead to complications, particularly if the

person is unable to explain what they are hearing.

Though equipment like noise-canceling headphones may assist, you may want to take further efforts to ensure your kid is comfortable at home. Here are some methods to adapt your house to eliminate annoying noises and the tension they might cause.

Address the Flooring
Replace hard flooring with noise-dampening carpeting. The sound of footfalls on hard surfaces may be extremely loud and upsetting to a person with autism. To soften the noise, choose carpet instead of wood, tile, or laminate floors.
Invest in a good-quality carpet pad. The cushion may lower the noise from the flooring, even more, so do not compromise on this area.

Use rugs to muffle noises on hard surfaces. If you require or prefer hard flooring, try utilizing area rugs to create a dampening effect on the surface. Soft textures absorb noises far better than hard surfaces.

Evaluate risk factors for falls. Falling at home is a problem for older persons and those with special needs who have balance or motor coordination challenges. Handrails and no-slip flooring may make a major impact.

Protect against Outdoor Noise Pollution
Protect your youngster from noises from the outside that might be distressing or interrupt sleep patterns. Remember that you may not hear all the noises that your youngster can hear. Whether it's everyday city noises or construction noise, it might influence your loved one with autism. Insulated windows are useful in blocking noise.

Install sound dampening insulation. Specially constructed insulation that dampens and absorbs noises may prevent those exterior sounds from entering your house.

Consider an additional layer of drywall if insulation is not viable. This will have the same effect as sound-dampening insulation and may be simpler to implement.

Be careful of the issue of echoing in wide, open settings. Though wide rooms may be beneficial for those with autism, they also cause echoes. These noises are unpleasant for autistic children, even if they are scarcely detectable to you. You can guard against this by adding soft textures to the floor and walls to lessen the echo. Strategically placed soft furniture might also help.

Focus on the autistic individual's bedroom first. If your budget does not allow you to complete all of the rooms in your house, make sure you insulate your autistic family member's bedroom first to lessen or eliminate outside noises.

Install thicker windows to dampen outdoor noise pollution. Look for windows with thick glass, laminated layers, and space between the window panes. Also, secondary glazing and specifically produced noise reduction glass are features that can help.

Additional Considerations for Noises at Home

Choose high-quality home audio equipment. The subtle differences in sound quality between different types of audio equipment can be painful for individuals with autism. Invest in higher quality equipment that produces good sound quality.

Understand that some individuals with autism will ignore sounds. This presents challenges of its own, because alarms in the home, such as smoke detectors or CO alarms, may be ignored. Consider investing in visual alarms if this is the case.

Reduce the Number of Smells in Your Home
Like the sense of touch and the sense of hearing, an autistic individual's sense of smell can be stronger than that of a neurotypical individual. Sometimes, scents and odors can trigger meltdowns or distress, even when they seem mild to other members of the family. There are measures you can take to reduce the input from smells in your home, particularly when you are remodeling to make it more autism-friendly. Here are some considerations to keep in mind.

Choose Low-Odor Finishes and Building Supplies
Understand the role of volatile organic compounds on your home and its occupants. VOCs are gases that solids and liquids emit in your home, and many finishes, including paints and varnishes,

contain VOCs. These are items that individuals with autism can be highly sensitive to, and the lingering odors are noticed long after neurotypical family members no longer smell them.

Choose low VOC paints and varnishes. These items will have less odor than their traditional counterparts. Using them will help keep the individual with autism calmer during the home renovations.

Choose low-odor building materials when performing home modifications. Paints and varnishes are not the only items that can have VOCs or other types of odors. Flooring, boards, drywall, and adhesives all contain odors as well. When possible, choose low-odor options. When not possible provide ample time for the space to air out with fresh air to remove the odors.

Opt for natural fibers instead of synthetic. Natural materials tend to have fewer offensive odors than synthetic materials, so choose them when possible. Even if it does have an odor, it will be from non-toxic materials, which will be easier for the individual with autism to process.

Add Proper Ventilation

Invest in proper ventilation for the home. Ventilation will reduce not only the home's odors from the renovation project but also the general odors in a home including cooking smells. Choose ventilation mechanisms that are properly insulated to protect from noise pollution.

Use HEPA filtration methods. Invest in certified HEPA filters for your home's HVAC system to further remove and neutralize VOCs and other odors.

Avoid air fresheners and chemical scents. Air fresheners and candles can add more confusion to your autistic family member's sensory input, so avoid adding them to the home environment while you seek to battle odors.

Make the Home Tactile-Friendly

The sense of touch is something that affects many people with autism intensely. Some find themselves overly sensitive to textures and things they can feel, while others find themselves craving tactile input. Some individuals with autism will experience both of these intensities. This is one area where home modifications can make a big difference. By creating touch-friendly spaces in your home, you can make it more inviting and calming for an autistic child or adult who lives there.

Focus on Textures

Add a variety of textures into the space. This can help those who are sensory-seeking find ways to self-calm. Add textures in furnishings, floor coverings, wall coverings, and accessories added to the home. Be aware that individuals with autism may have strong aversions to specific textures, so be sensitive to your loved one's unique needs.

Remove and replace textures the individual finds upsetting. If something is too rough or too smooth, remove it from the environment and replace it with something more tolerable.

Make the Home Durable
Understand that children with autism are going to touch everything. Make sure your home is friendly to this type of behavior. Remove items that could be broken by a pair of curious hands.

Prepare for repetitive behaviors by purchasing durable materials and furnishings. One of the common traits of autism is repetitive behaviors. Closing the same door over and over, walking the same path repeatedly, or stimming in a certain area of the home are all possibilities. Make sure your home can stand up to these types of repeated behaviors.

Bring Nature Indoors
Add plants that are safe for the individual to interact with. Houseplants and an indoor garden can soothe individuals with autism and bring part of nature indoors, which is calming. This also provides something else to touch and feel. Be cautious about potentially poisonous plants, because individuals with autism may wish to interact with plants differently than neurotypical people do.

Make space for a sensory garden outdoors. Bringing nature inside is a good idea, but it does have its limits. Plant a sensory garden outdoors that will stimulate all five senses, and allow the autistic family member to spend time in the garden often.

Assess Tactile Challenges in the Bathroom

Understand the challenges the traditional bathroom creates. Cold toilet seats, harsh cleaning chemicals, slippery floors, and poor ventilation can make bathrooms challenging areas for individuals with autism. Focus on home modifications that reduce these risks. Some are simple, like adding a cushioned toilet seat or soft, warm rug, while others may require some actual home modification.

Add non-slip surfaces to the tub and bathroom floors. When individuals with autism struggle with balance and the vestibular system, slippery floors are dangerous. Add non-slip surfaces too slick bathroom and tub floors.

Improve ventilation in the bathroom. Poor ventilation can make bathrooms smelly, which makes them uncomfortable spaces for individuals with autism. Invest in better ventilation. If the bathroom is on an outside wall, consider adding a window to improve the comfort of the space.

Create a water play area, because individuals with autism are naturally drawn to water. Water plan is another favorite activity for many individuals with autism. Make the bathroom a place where water play is safe. Consider installing a floor drain and protecting surfaces in the bathroom in case the individual with autism chooses to play in the faucet or tub.

Add safety features to the bathroom like grab bars. Again, when individuals with autism struggle with the balance due to vestibular system concerns, having something to grab can be helpful.

General Considerations for Your Home
Children and adults on the autism spectrum, as well as others with sensory processing concerns, need special considerations at home to help them with their sensory processing and overall functioning. Some home modifications do not fit into categories for specific senses, like taste or

hearing. However, these modifications can make a tremendous difference to a child or adult who is battling over-stimulating environments.

Create a Sensory Room
Build a room that has the sensory materials your child needs. These are very helpful for families who have autistic family members as they provide a place to meet sensory needs that are different than the neurotypical population. What your home's sensory room contains will be unique to the needs of your child or family member.

Add a swing to the room. Swinging is quite calming for individuals with autism and can help with the self-regulation of senses and emotions. Safely mount a swing in your sensory room by mounting it to a ceiling joist. Make sure the swing is strong enough to handle different weights, so it can be used by a young child as well as an adult. A hammock can also help with this need. Add play equipment that allows for large motor movement. Rocking, sliding, and jumping are all movements that individuals with autism sometimes crave. Find out what your child or loved one needs, then add the furniture and equipment that will allow them to safely engage in these behaviors. A small indoor trampoline, indoor slide, or rocking furniture can all be helpful additions to a sensory room. If you do not have the space for these, consider exercise balls, bouncy seats, and similar small items that allow for proprioceptive input and large motor movement.

Install or purchase furniture that allows for deep pressure. Bean bags and similar furniture that a child or autistic adult can pile on and around themselves can help create a calming sensory experience that is helpful for those with autism. Deep pressure is important for individuals with autism that crave sensory input or who have proprioceptive sensory needs.

Add a ball pit. Ball pits are a helpful sensory experience for those with autism, and they can be installed in a sensory room. If the budget is limited, you can use an inflatable pool with balls inside for the same effect.

Add a variety of calm, soothing lighting options. In addition to the regular overhead lighting in the space, add mood lighting, twinkling Christmas lights, spotlights, and more to create the right ambiance. Ensure that the room has the right electrical breaker service to support these lights.
Install an air conditioner. The addition of extra lights can make the room hot, and that can be unbearable to an individual with autism. Install a room air conditioner to compensate.

Fill the room with tactile and sensory items, but keep it organized. It is easy for a sensory room to become overstimulating if too many items are added without proper organization. Use shelving and bins to add tactile and sensory items in an organized, uncluttered way.

Build a climbing wall. A climbing wall is also an important tool in a sensory room for individuals with autism who are prone to climbing furniture. Build one to give a safe place for climbing inside your home.

Turn your child's bedroom into the sensory room if another space is not available. Sometimes you won't have room in your home to make a separate sensory room. If this is the case, build these ideas into your autistic child or loved one's bedroom.

Create a sensory corner. Another option if a dedicated room is not available is to create a sensory corner that contains many of the sensory input items. To help the individual with autism block out the sounds and visual impact of the rest of the home, use noise-canceling headphones and physical barriers to a portion of this part of the room.

Build a Cool-Down Room
Build a cool-down room if the autistic individual is prone to meltdowns. This provides a safe place to have the meltdown where the child and the home will not be damaged, even if the behaviors turn violent. This can be part of the sensory room but often is better as a separate space.

Strengthen the windows in the cool-down room. This will prevent windows from being broken amid a meltdown.

Add soft mats to the walls and flooring so the individual with autism can safely crash into them. This can have a calming effect in the middle of a meltdown. Sensory crash pads also help with proprioceptive input, which is necessary for people with autism

Ensure all objects in the room, including furniture, are soft or have softened edges. If the child is experiencing violent movements during a meltdown, this will add protection.

Control lighting through a dimmer switch. Lower lighting may be important during a meltdown, but may not be necessary at all times in this room.

Hang drapes, not blinds, and use Velcro instead of curtain rods. This will prevent damage to the walls if the child pulls on the window coverings.

Invest in a Generator
Purchase and install a generator. Power outages can disrupt the routine of your home and eliminate the electronic devices that can be soothing to your autistic loved one. Installing a generator ensures that you always have access to these items, even if you lose power.

Use the generator to keep up with the routine. Having your routine stay the same, even during an electrical power outage, is critical to helping your autistic loved one stay comfortable at home.

Consider Important Safety Concerns
Individuals with autism, particularly children, require additional protections that may not be a concern for the neurotypical world. When considering home modifications for autistic family members, make sure to consider safety amid the other considerations and changes you make. From protecting your autistic child from wandering to ensuring the flooring is safe, there are steps you can take to protect your loved one from some of the challenges that neurodiversity can bring.

Concerns About Wandering
Understand that individuals with autism sometimes wander away from home. In one study, nearly half of parents with autistic

children indicated their child had tried to wander away from home after the age of four, and of those, 53 percent were missing long enough to make the parents worried. An additional 65 percent involved close calls with vehicles. Wandering is a serious safety risk for individuals with autism, with children being at particularly high risk.

Install fencing so children with autism can play outdoors safely. Individuals with autism, including children, often enjoy being outdoors. However, the tendency to wander can make outdoor play dangerous. Protect your child by installing a fence with a locking gate, and ensuring that the gate's lock is inaccessible to the child.

Choose fencing that adds a visual barrier. Sometimes the distractions of other people's homes and yards can detract from the enjoyment of the outdoors, so choose privacy fencing that adds a visual barrier from these distractions.

Select fencing that cannot be climbed. Children who want to wander may climb chain links and even many types of wood fencing. Choose fencing options that are too slick to climb, and avoid placing outdoor toys close enough to the fencing to provide a climbing opportunity.

Use proximity alarms and doorway alarms to alert caretakers when an individual with autism tries to leave the home. Install alarms on all doors that will provide an instant alert if the door is opened without permission, so you can stop your loved one from wandering before a serious event occurs.

Install door chimes over all doors if an alarm system is not possible. This is an inexpensive way to give yourself an alert if your child or autistic loved one leaves the home.

Add extra locks to the doors. In addition to deadbolts, install key-based locks and ensure that doors be secured at all times. Remember that persons with autism are typically good at opening locks, so use various kinds. Flip locks are also effective for decreasing the chance of straying.
Install locks or barriers on windows. Autistic children may jump out of windows, therefore put tamper-proof locks or other obstacles on windows to reduce this danger.

Install slanted window sills to discourage climbing. This may stop youngsters from attempting to climb up to or out of windows. Consider building a self-contained apartment inside your house for a young adult with special needs. Some children with autism are not able to leave home when they reach maturity. However, you may be able to offer them some greater freedom while keeping them securely under your roof.

Concerns about Burns and Scalding

Reduce the danger of burns and scalding. persons with autism with their enhanced sense of touch might be more prone to pain from high temperatures.

Lower the water heater temperature. You may need to adjust the water heater temperature below the suggested levels to minimize pain for your autistic loved one. Keep the water temperature at 120 degrees or below to prevent scorching or burns.

Protect the water heater against tampering. Whether you lock the basement or put a barrier around the water heater, be sure the autistic family member cannot modify the water heater temperature.

Add locks on stove knobs. Make sure the person with autism cannot operate the stove knobs unless the individual is high functioning enough to cook safely.

Consider adding an induction cooktop. Induction cooktops do not generate a heated surface. This might be the safest cooktop for a household with a person with autism since it is nearly impossible to burn your hands by touching the stove. Also, if the person with autism turns the cooktop on and leaves it on, the fire danger is negligible.

Protect Children from Furniture

Tether bookcases and other furniture to the wall to prevent them from tipping. Autistic children may climb furniture that others would leave alone, and if the furniture is not fastened securely to the wall, it might tumble over and damage or kill the kid. Falling furniture is a danger to all children, but because of the way autistic children engage with the environment around them, it may be a higher risk to these kids.

Install built-in storage wherever feasible. This further decreases the possibility of having the furniture tilt onto the infant.

Mount media equipment to the wall at a high height. A media center is a tipping danger since enormous TVs may easily tumble off of a shelf or entertainment center. Mount them firmly on the wall instead.

Remember to fasten dressers to the wall as well. Dressers may easily topple over, especially when all of the drawers are opened. Use wall mounting solutions to safeguard your autistic loved one.

Use two anchors for securing furniture to the wall. If one anchor breaks or if it is not strong enough to keep the furniture secure, you will have a backup piece.
Install anchors into wall studs or solid wood. Anchors may come out of drywall or

particle board very easily, so be sure they are secured firmly.

Protect Children from Drowning
Understand that many autistic children are captivated by water. Because of this, all sources of water need to be shielded from the youngster. This covers swimming pools as well as toilets and baths.

Add a fence around any outdoor pools, lakes, or bodies of water. Even though the water appears shallow, it must be gated to effectively safeguard an autistic youngster. Remember, all it takes is an inch of water for a kid to drown, and autistic children are attracted to water.

Install a pool alarm. A pool alarm will inform you if someone, like your autistic loved one, slips into the pool accidentally. If you have a backyard pool, you must have a pool alarm.

Additional Safety Considerations

Protect your youngster from self-injury during head bashing. Many persons with autism may stim, which refers to doing repeated motions that assist relax and quieting an individual with autism. Some forms of stims, including head pounding, have the potential to produce damage. Provide an area in the house where these stims may take place. If you discover that your autistic kid or loved one has a favorite area to stimulate, make that place safe by adding cushions and padding.

Consider any additional self-injuring activities. Each person with autism is unique, and the potentially self-injuring behaviors that one individual experiences will be different for another one. If you identify self-injuring habits that the home environment may assist prevent, make the required modifications.

Install locks on all unsafe storage spaces. Medicines, household cleansers, sharp things, devices that might be harmful, and other family members' areas should all be secured and unavailable to give an extra degree of safety. Keep in mind that basic childproof locks may not be adequate to effectively safeguard autistic children from these threats.

Add plexiglass over TVs and photo frames. Shattered glass is a severe safety issue, therefore safeguard your things and your autistic loved one from this risk.

Consider adding security cameras. If self-injury or roaming are severe issues, security cameras may provide caregivers piece of mind while they consider the best interests of their autistic loved ones. This will provide you a tool to utilize to enable your autistic loved one with some freedom inside the house, without compromising safety. You can constantly check in on what they are doing, even while granting them a bit of freedom.

Take additional steps during remodeling or construction, when standard protections may not be in place. Home renovations might interrupt your typical routines and bring additional hazards to your loved one with autism. Be extremely vigilant during these periods and identify potential hazards.

chapter five

Discipline Strategies for Children With Autism

When a child misbehaves, whether the problematic behavior is throwing a temper tantrum, hitting another kid, or ignoring instructions, you may be inclined to scold them or take away certain privileges. But disciplining a child with autism may require a different approach.

Traditional discipline techniques aren't always effective for a child with autism. Depending on where they fall on the spectrum, they might struggle to understand the consequences or handle harsh reprimands. But that doesn't mean you shouldn't use any discipline at all. Instead, gentler and consistent strategies may be the key to helping children with autism manage their behavior.

How to Manage Misbehavior Without Punishment

Understanding Common Autistic Behaviors

We usually discipline children because they consciously act in inappropriate ways, whether it's swiping treats off a sibling's plate or intentionally tripping a child on the soccer field. However, a child with autism may not be able to control certain behaviors, and they mustn't be harshly punished for them. Some behaviors that children with autism may struggle to control include:

Biting their hands and fingers

Hand flapping or rocking (self-stimulating behavior that helps people with autism regulate their emotions)

Screaming or yelling

Hurting themselves by banging or hitting their heads

Not looking at people or making eye contact

Physical aggression toward peers and grown-ups, like biting or kicking

Many of these behaviors stem from children's struggles to express their needs or desires or understand social norms and cues.1 You shouldn't place your child in time-out, shame them, or spank them because of these behaviors. Rather, you must work to better understand why they are acting out in this way and, if necessary, try to avoid those triggers in the future.

 What Is Gentle Discipline?
Use Positive Reinforcement
Children with autism respond better to discipline techniques that focus on the positive. With positive reinforcement strategies, you call attention to things your child is doing right (using their quiet voice in the supermarket, for example) and praise them or reward them for it.

Some children might be motivated by a classic sticker chart, where they can collect stickers for good behavior and eventually earn a prize for a certain number of stickers.

But many children with autism, particularly young ones, respond to more immediate positive feedback and rewards that relate directly to the behavior. For example, if they ask nicely for a stuffed animal in a store rather than scream or hit their heads in frustration, they earn immediate praise (and maybe, if appropriate, the stuffed animal).

 How Praise Can Promote Good Behavior
Teach Self-Calming Techniques
Meltdowns are common in kids, but it can be harder to calm a child with autism. Some children with autism can learn self-calming techniques for when they start to feel out of control of themselves or a situation.

One simple self-calming technique they can try is to breathe in and out through their nose slowly while closing their eyes and imagining something pleasant, like their kitty or their favorite park. If you or another trusted adult is around, they can hug the adult until they're settled. Gentle, steady pressure, like a hug, is calming for many children with autism.

Control Their Environment
For children with autism especially, it's helpful to make their immediate environment conducive to their comfort. Taking care to fill their play area or room with preferred toys and objects can make them feel more safe and comfortable, which may lead to more regulated behavior.

Conversely, try to avoid situations that you know can trigger their agitation—for some kids with autism, for example, it can be crowded or noisy places—and be on the lookout for signs of pending frustration. Sometimes, kids with autism can be compulsive about certain toys or activities and that can interfere with basic routines.[1] These distractions can be removed when tasks need to be completed.

Stick to Routines

Many kids with autism crave consistency and order and can struggle to cope when regular routines are disrupted.2 They might lash out or increase self-stimulating behaviors to deal with unpredictable situations. Help them by limiting the number of activities you have them do and sticking to a predictable schedule.

That might mean skipping a speech therapy session one week rather than bumping it to another day when the teacher is accidentally double booked, or not trying to fit in sudden, unexpected errands with them after a long day of school. Create a schedule that you can display in your child's room or a common area with pictures they can use to quickly identify what they can expect to do each day of the week (like a photo of their speech therapist on Tuesday).

Communicate Clearly
It's best to use plain language and directives with kids who have autism. Children with

autism spectrum disorders often have trouble understanding subtleties in verbal language or body language.

When your child starts acting out, direct them to what you prefer them to do rather than what they shouldn't do. For example, if a child is pulling a dog's tail, don't say, "Stop hurting the dog." Instead, you can say, "Pet the dog softly."

Ignore Harmless Behaviors
Some behaviors of children with autism seem strange but aren't dangerous or disruptive. Primary examples of this are self-stimulating behaviors like hand-flapping or rocking.

If a problem behavior occurs infrequently, doesn't prevent your family or others from regular routines, and doesn't harm your child or others, then it should be ignored whenever possible.1

Put Safety First

Many children with autism don't display behavior that would hurt themselves or others. However, whenever you are dealing with a behavioral situation in which a child is physically lashing out, you need to make sure that they (and others around them) are safe.

If your child is having a tantrum that is hard to stop, be sure to remove hard or sharp objects that might be in their path. If you are having trouble removing your child from a populated place (such as the playground or a birthday party), recruit help from another grown-up to distract and direct other children to another area.

Seek Professional Help

If you are finding it hard to manage your child's behavior, don't hesitate to seek professional help. Look for people with expertise in helping children with autism, like developmental-behavioral pediatricians or child psychologists.

Several therapies have been proven to be helpful for kids with autism. Most stem from the principles of applied behavioral analysis (ABA), which focuses on building and encouraging new skills, providing access to preferred activities and toys, giving kids choices whenever possible, increasing appropriate communication, and making complex situations more predictable using signals and other routine gestures.

The purpose of discipline is to set healthy boundaries and clear expectations of appropriate behavior, not to punish or embarrass your child.

While there are certainly challenges to disciplining a child on the autism spectrum, discipline instills valuable lessons that the child will take with them their whole lives. Keep reading to learn safe, effective, and compassionate strategies for how to discipline a child on the autism spectrum.

Two Words: Gentle Consistency
Children with autism pick up on things differently than other children. For example, your child may not pick up on the irritation in your voice when you ask them not to do something.

These misunderstandings can make traditional discipline techniques less effective. Your child might not understand the consequences of their actions, which can be frustrating. However, you should refrain from any kind of physical or verbal punishment that could hurt your child.

Instead, be gentle with your words and actions. If your child is screaming and having a tantrum, keep calm and don't raise your voice. All children learn through imitation, so try and respond to your child's behavior clearly and gently.

And now for consistency. Consistency is the key to safe, effective discipline. Most children with autism respond well to structured discipline, perhaps due to their desire for sameness and routine.

Consistent discipline can also alleviate some of your child's anxiety, a common characteristic of autism. Consistent outcomes help children feel secure and confident in their choices.

If your child knows what to expect from a certain behavior (Mom won't like that I ate cookies before dinner), they may not feel as overwhelmed when you discipline them.

In other words, consistency gives your child the ability to predict the outcome of a situation, which is a powerful and necessary step toward independence.

Educate Yourself About Your Child's Condition

You'll need to do some research before fully understanding how to discipline a child on the autism spectrum.

Read up on the condition to make sure you're setting realistic expectations for your child. Some behaviors cannot be "disciplined away" by a parent, and should instead be evaluated by a professional.

For example, self-stimulation (spinning, hand flapping, etc.) is very common in children with autism. These behaviors help them regulate their emotions, and you could do more harm than good by punishing them for doing it.

Remember that autism exists on a spectrum, meaning every child will experience different symptoms in different ways. It's a good idea to speak with other parents whose children have autism. You'll get a better idea of how to set expectations, especially if you speak with a parent whose child has symptoms similar to yours.

The goal of rewards and consequences is to increase or decrease the likelihood of your child performing a certain behavior. When your child performs the desired behavior or task, you offer them a "reward" – a positive reinforcer.

When they do not perform the desired behavior or task, you point them in the right direction with a consequence.

For example, you can offer your child candy or extra TV time for cleaning their room after being asked. That is an example of a positive reinforcer. If they don't clean their room after being asked, you can take away some of their TV time or send them to time-out. That is the consequence.

Of course, you'll have to evaluate which consequences are appropriate for your child. For instance, some children with autism prefer being alone, so sending them to time out could be a reward for them.

Set Clear Expectations
Children with autism often have trouble understanding which behaviors are expected of them. For example, a child may not understand that they should say "hello" back to someone who greets them.

You can help your child learn these behaviors by clearly communicating your expectations. You may need to create visual cues or do role-playing until your child is comfortable.

For example, if your child is late getting ready every morning because they're playing with their toys, you can explain that they can play only after they are ready for school. You can set a timer showing your child how much time is left before they need to leave for school, and after they finish getting ready, they can play until the timer runs out.

Be Positive

Positivity inspires positive actions. If you offer praise and encouragement when your child behaves well, they'll want to keep behaving well.

Encourage your child by reminding them what they can earn or receive for meeting their goals. Praise your child when they perform good behavior, and describe exactly what it is you're praising. This is called "descriptive praise," and it helps children understand appropriate and inappropriate behavior. For example, "Great job asking Dylan nicely for your toy when he took it from you."

You can also praise children for their efforts, not just the final result.

Most children with autism enjoy praise, but some may not respond, especially if they tend to withdraw from others. They probably aren't motivated or interested in doing things to please other people, so you can help your child learn how to respond to praise. You can tell them what they did well and then give them their favorite toy. This way, they'll come to regard praise as something good.

Discipling a Child on the Autism Spectrum
Discipline teaches children to do the right thing and think and act for themselves. It can be difficult to discipline a child who has autism, but doing so will help teach them the skills they need to live an independent life.

9 798845 637321